Leisure Arts 29

Painting
Landscapes in
Acrylics

Wendy Clouse

SEARCH PRESS

Introduction – Acrylics

Acrylic is an ideal medium for the landscape painter because it allows the freedom to paint in many techniques. It can be used like gouache or in the traditional oil techniques (using water, of course, in place of turpentine). Acrylic can also be used as a watercolour medium in either the traditional technique, or wet-in-wet. When used as watercolour it has the advantage of allowing the painter to lay one wash over the other without disturbing the previous one. The greatest advantage that acrylic possesses over other mediums, however, lies in its speed of drying and also in the fact that, once it is dry, it is permanent. Mistakes can quickly be remedied by painting over. Doing this in oils is messy, and in watercolour almost impossible.

The aim of this book is to demonstrate how acrylic can be used in all of these different techniques.

Materials and equipment

To me there are few occasions as enjoyable or exciting as a warm sunny day in the English countryside, when I can set up my easel, paint to my heart's content, and be at peace with the world. This does not happen very often, unfortunately. Not only do we have the weather to contend with, but flies, mosquitoes, curious people, curious cows, not to mention traffic. Another problem is the amount of equipment or clothes one needs for a day's painting. I have frequently seen people set out on a landscape painting trip so laden that they were lucky to get as far as their front gate.

My suggestion is to take a small rucksack/backpack. Into this, put only the tubes of colour you need for the day – eight should be enough. The colours I suggest are burnt sienna, yellow ochre, cadmium red, alizarin crimson, lemon yellow, ultramarine blue, Prussian blue, and sap green. Pack them loose – wooden boxes just add extra weight. Take no more than three brushes, two or three soft rags, and squash bottles. These, in the normal or small size, are ideal for carrying water and also, cut in half, make ideally light water pots. You will need two of these pots, one pencil, and one rubber. It is a good idea to take two small canvasses or boards as you may wish to begin a second painting while the first is drying, or are enjoying yourself so much that, having finished the first painting, you decide to stay and start another. Make sure, however, that your boards or canvas or paper are no larger than your rucksack. It is much easier to carry all you need in one bag.

You will also, of course, need a small palette, I suggest one of the disposable kind. If you also take along a small plastic bag, at the end of the day's painting you can tear off the disposable used palette sheet and pop it into your bag to take home and throw away. For that matter, even during the day you may want a clean palette. In addition, a few sheets of sketch paper or a small sketch pad will be of great use, as I explain later (page 7).

Besides your art materials it is usually sensible to take along an extra sweater, a plastic raincoat (these can be purchased in a tiny bag), insect repellant, and suntan lotion. Sandwiches and a flask of coffee are pleasant, some would say vital, extras. All of these items well packed will fit into quite a small backpack.

When everything is packed, a light canvas stool should just fit over the top before you close the bag. The flap will then hold it in place.

All that you have left to carry now is an easel – a wooden or metal portable one is best – and you can buy shoulder bags too to put those in. Even with your backpack in place and easel under or over your arm, distance should be no problem and you will still be able to open (and close) gates or climb over stiles.

Note. In this book only five colours are used, burnt sienna, ultramarine blue, yellow ochre, cadmium red and sap green, apart from white. It is better when painting to use a minimum of colours, a limited palette. This allows the painter truly to understand his colours and what they can do. Also, a painting with few colours will hold together better compositionally, whereas a painting containing many colours may appear busy and fragmented.

'...lucky to get as far as the front gate'.

Distant village: demonstration (pages 4-5)

Acrylic paint used as watercolour in the traditional technique

Size: 27cm × 17½cm (10¾in. × 7in.)
Paper: Hot pressed (smooth) watercolour paper
Colours: Yellow ochre, cadmium red, ultramarine blue, sap green and burnt sienna.
Brushes: nos. 16 and 7 watercolour brushes

With traditional watercolour, the painter always has to be fast and careful when applying a second wash so as not to remove parts of the previous one. Using acrylic as watercolour is especially advantageous as, once the acrylic is dry, the next wash will not disturb it.

In this painting I try to show how a difficult subject, or panorama, can be simplified. This is best done by cutting down on detail. To do this, look at your subject with half-closed eyes, so that you see only the more important details. Look through your viewfinder (see page 6); it will help you to decide which parts of the scene to paint and where the edges of your painting will be. Try to select some principal object – a church, mountain, lake or, as here, a distant village – to give focus and interest to the painting.

Stages 1 and 2 (page 4)

The sketch is drawn with a 2B pencil, after which a wash of yellow ochre is applied to dry paper. The first brush stroke of the wash is taken straight across the middle of the painting at the horizon level. It is then washed to the top of the paper, the colour being gradually diluted. This is called a graded wash. The same technique is applied to the bottom half of the picture. When acrylics are used as a watercolour medium, as with traditional watercolours, white paint is not employed. For white areas the white paper is saved and for light colour the pigment is watered down.

After the first stage has dried, the sky is painted. Here I use a mixture of ultramarine blue and cadmium red, stronger at the top of the painting and graded down to the horizon by dilution with water. The whole

Stage 1

Stage 2

Stage 3

Stage 4

sky area should not be covered but parts of the yellow ochre left to show through, to allow light shapes for clouds.

Stage 3

I find it easier to paint landscapes in this sequence: first the sky, then the distance, next the middle ground, and finally the foreground, as if I were walking from the back (distance) to the front (foreground) of the picture, painting each area as I arrive at it. This way I find it

easier to save the strongest values (darkest darks) for the foreground. Also, objects that are supposed to be behind seem much more convincing than those which are awkwardly fitted in.

For the background trees, pylons and the church spires I make a watered-down mixture of sap green and ultramarine blue. I apply it as a flat wash, for distance offers no detail. The houses are painted with a mixture of cadmium red and burnt sienna, the shadows in the same colour but with a little ultramarine blue added.

Stage 5 – the finished painting

Stage 4

Now the middle ground. I paint yellow ochre over the background colour for the distant corn fields, and a stronger mixture of ultramarine blue and sap green for the village trees. I add roofs to the houses with a mixture of ultramarine blue and burnt sienna. The field colour is sap green plus yellow ochre.

Stage 5 – the finished painting (page 5)

The closer trees and hedge are painted in two values. I allow the light wash to dry, then I add the darker value. I use a mixture of sap green, ultramarine blue and burnt sienna. The foreground field I paint in sap green and, while it is still wet (damp), drop in burnt sienna and ultramarine blue. Finally I apply cadmium red for the poppies.

Landscape painting – how to start

There is nothing more terrifying to the beginner-painter than going out into the countryside to paint for the first time. Everywhere one looks there are scenes just waiting to be painted; but everything also seems so vast compared to one's little canvas, and there is so much interesting subject-matter available that it is difficult to decide what to paint.

My suggestion is to make a small viewfinder, very similar to the ones that photographic slides come in, only perhaps rather larger (see sketch), to act as a frame. Hold the viewfinder in front of your eyes, look

through it, and scan the area until you light upon a subject or area that interests you. Next, still looking through the viewfinder, bring it first closer, then push it further away from you (to act like a telescopic lens on a camera) until you can decide how best to frame or compose your painting, and whether you want your subject, for example, close up or in the distance.

Remember, however, if you are not very experienced, to begin with simple subjects which demand few colours, for example a stile, a tree, a country lane or a fence in the hedge. Simple subjects such as these can, I assure you, make delightful paintings.

When you have selected a subject it is a good idea to make a few thumbnail sketches, approximately 10cm by 7.5cm or 4in. by 3in. This way, by the time you begin the actual painting, you will know your subject well, and feel at ease with it. This preparation will also help to eliminate too much rubbing out and beginning again.

Always, by the way, keep a sketch book with you so that when there is no time to paint, you can make a quick sketch. Used in the studio on a rainy day, with a little creativity, these sketches can be turned into paintings, often much larger than you would attempt in the open air.

Reflections: demonstration (pages 8-9)

Acrylic used as watercolour in the wet-in-wet technique

Size: 27cm × 17½cm (10¾in. × 7in.)
Paper: rough watercolour paper, 140lb
Colours used: ultramarine blue, burnt sienna, sap green, yellow ochre, cadmium red light
Brushes: nos. 16 and 7, with fine points

Water is endlessly fascinating as subject-matter, and many people find landscapes which include it both serene and peaceful. Ponds and rivers constantly attract artists but many, when beginning to paint, shy away because they find it difficult to paint water. The important thing to remember is to forget about the surface and to look deeper. Squint your eyes. Look for the large light or dark shapes, the colourful patchwork that reflects sky and landscape. Put it together like a jigsaw puzzle, add a few horizontal ripples, and the water is painted.

Stage 1 (page 8)
I begin by making a sketch in 2B pencil. When this is completed I soak the paper thoroughly with clean water, the water being applied with a large watercolour wash brush. The paper is then left to absorb the water, until the shine has gone off. At this stage a small amount of burnt sienna is mixed with ultramarine blue to paint the sky and the reflections of the sky in the water.
Note. Whenever you paint with acrylics it is important either to wash out brushes well after each use or, more sensibly, to keep them in jar of water during the actual painting and wash them well afterwards.

Stage 2
Working quickly, and while the paper is still damp, I mix a more equal mixture of burnt sienna and ultramarine blue to produce a grey, and apply this to the areas of shadow in the painting.

Stage 1

Stage 2

Stage 3

Stage 4

Stage 3

If I work fast enough, my paper remains damp. If I do not, it does not greatly matter, for here is one of the advantages of acrylic over watercolour. If the paper is almost dry, I let it dry completely and then re-wet it all over, as before, and wait until I have the required dampness. Once acrylic paint is dry it is impossible to remove it whereas, if this painting had been executed in watercolour, re-wetting would be virtually impossible.

I now paint the background trees, and the hedges in front of the house, with sap green to which I add a little ultramarine blue. The hedge on the right and the grassy bank are done in pure sap green while I use yellow ochre for the grass on the right.

Stage 5 – the finished painting

Stage 4

At this stage I have allowed the painting to dry completely before adding a mixture of cadmium red light and burnt sienna to the brick building and the chimney pots. Also I have mixed ultramarine blue and burnt sienna to form a grey that is suitable for the tiled roof. I have added too a second value to some of the green areas while all of this, of course, is repeated in the watery reflection.

Stage 5 – the finished painting

Up till this point, I have used only the no.16 brush. Now I take the no.7 brush to paint details, windows and ledges, ripples in the water, and to add a few strokes to the dry grass on the right.

Trees

Trees tend to be the most prevalent objects in landscape paintings, but they are also the most difficult to draw and paint. It is seldom indeed that we see a landscape painting without some trees or brushes – even the desert has scrub bushes and low gnarled trees. It is very important, therefore, for the landscape painter to gain as much experience as possible in drawing and painting trees. Carry a sketchbook with you, so that whenever you are in the country, or having your lunch break outdoors or in the park, you can spend a few minutes studying the texture of the trunk, the bole (the area where all the main branches leave the trunk) or the shape of the tree as a whole. These studies will prove to be invaluable later when you are completing a landscape painting.

Study the trees in the distance, see how they seem then, as I mention under 'Perspective' (page 14), to be of one value, or one flat colour. This is especially noticeable on a misty morning when the distant landscape appears in flat layers, each closer layer being slightly darker than the previous one, and all not very different from the colour of the sky.

Trees in the middle distance will be more detailed, branches possibly showing and foliage appearing in two values (light and dark) instead of a single one as in distant trees.

The time spent studying trees proves to be of greatest value, of course, when painting them into the foreground of a picture; for here all the painting of trunks, branches and foliage is at its strongest both in detail and in colour. (*See also pages 12–13 and 32.*)

13

Perspective in landscape painting

The word perspective can be a frightening concept to someone who is still learning to paint; and some students at first find perspective a total mystery. In landscape painting, however, perspective is less of a problem than it is, for instance, in drawing buildings. There is less need to worry about linear perspective, rather the need is to concentrate on *aerial* perspective – receding colours and tonal values which create the illusion of space and depth.

The atmosphere through which we view the landscape is filled with particles of dust and water vapour. These will seem to cast a blue-grey veil over distant objects, and even over not-so-distant objects. As a result they dull the colour and also reduce surface detail. Colour changes, therefore, as much as do lines and shapes. Accordingly distant hills, mountains, and, as I have shown, trees will appear to become lighter the further away they are; and very bright colours will look lighter and hazier in the distance.

I have painted in 'Summer fields' (pages 16-17) a simple landscape with trees in order to demonstrate the effects of aerial perspective. In the distance the trees are small, en masse, a flat cool grey in colour, and with no detail.

In the middleground I have added a little green to the grey colour and have painted the trees and bushes in two values, light and dark – not a bright light or a strong dark, however, as I will need these tones for the trees in the foreground. Here I have painted in full colour and used three values – light, middle tone and dark. By using aerial perspective I have created an illusion of depth and space on my paper or canvas.

When painting landscape, of course, it is vital to consider the weather. It is of no use to paint the sky grey to portray a cloudy wet day and then to paint the rest of the picture in bright colours as if it were a sunny day! On a grey day all the colours must be toned down or made greyer. On a sunny day all colours will appear to be lighter and brighter.

Summer fields (pages 16-17)

Acrylic used in the traditional oil-painting technique

Size: 37½cm × 26cm (15in. × 10½in.)
Paper: Fine grain oil-painting paper
Brushes: nos. 8, 4 hog-hair oil

This painting demonstrates the effects of light on the landscape. To me it portrays a typical English landscape on a hot summer day, the sun intermittently shining and with heavy haze in the distance. It also demonstrates, as I have described, aerial perspective.

First I give the canvas a covering of yellow ochre. When this is dry I make my sketch (see below), block in all the colours, and then begin to paint more thickly and in more detail. I paint the sky first, followed by background, middle ground and, last, foreground.

As I complete the painting I find that, because the background is too strong, it does not give enough depth to the picture. So I mix a small amount of ultramarine blue with a little white, water it right down and use this

continued from page 15

as a glaze to veil and therefore to lighten my background. A glaze is a thin, transparent wash of paint which is laid over other colours to tone them down or bring them forward.

Finally, to bring the foreground forward, I make a very watery mixture of lemon yellow and cadmium red (orange) and lay a transparent glaze over the foreground to brighten it.

The colours I use in this painting are yellow ochre, white, burnt sienna, ultramarine blue, sap green, and a very small amount of cadmium red in my foreground glaze.

'Summer Fields' aims to demonstrate both the effect of light on the landscape, and aerial perspective.

Surrey lane in winter: demonstration

Acrylic paint used in traditional oil-painting technique

Size: 27cm × 17½cm (10¾in. × 7in.)
Paper: Fine grain oil-painting paper
Brushes: nos. 8 and 4 oil brushes; no. 1 rigger (a watercolour brush with extra long bristles)
Colours used: ultramarine blue, burnt sienna, cadmium red, sap green, yellow ochre, titanium white.

Stage 1 (page 19)

After making several thumbnail sketches, one of which is shown here, I select the viewpoint I prefer and draw it out on to my canvas. As I do so, I mark in the area where shadow will fall across the road.

Stage 2

Burnt sienna is diluted with water to colour my ground (painting surface). This can be done before the drawing or afterwards because, being a thin wash, it is transparent enough for the drawing to show through. Tinting the canvas both provides a warm background colour for the painting and helps with middle tones (lights and darks are easier to work out on a middle-tone background). When the burnt sienna ground has dried I go over my drawing to strengthen it with ultramarine blue, diluted.

Incidentally, up until the time of William Turner (1775–1851) landscapists generally worked on a warm dark background. Turner exploited this, at first, but with his innovative use of colour, his grounds became paler and his mature works were generally executed on a white ground.

Stage 3

Still keeping the paint thin, and working fairly loosely, I indicate the dark areas with a mixture of burnt sienna and ultramarine blue.

Stage 4

With the values (lights and darks) worked out I now begin to paint more thickly. The sky is painted with ultramarine blue with a little burnt sienna added, plus white. Notice that the brush strokes are not overworked or smoothed out, but left to create painterly texture and also to allow the warm ground to show through in places. The distant hills I paint with a slightly stronger mixture of the sky colour, while the trees to the right use the same two colours but this time with more burnt sienna. For the field I use a mixture of sap green and ultramarine blue.

continued on page 20

Stage 1

Stage 2

Stage 3

Stage 4

Stage 5 – the finished painting

Stage 5 – the finished painting

This painting took only about two hours to complete. Sometimes it is good to push oneself to paint quite quickly because it is more likely to produce a fresh and spontaneous effect.

To complete the picture I proceed from middle ground to foreground. For the fine twigs on the large tree I scumble a mixture of ultramarine blue and burnt sienna. Scumbling is a technique in which dry, thickish paint is applied to a surface in a loose, direct manner,

the side of the brush being dragged over the surface in different directions.

Of the colours on the palette I use for this painting (see colours listed) all are painted into the hedge and grass verge. Cadmium red, ultramarine blue, and white are used for the road. When this dries I spurtle paint from a stiff toothbrush to achieve texture. Spurtle, derived from the word 'spurt', is my word for describing what happens when paint is flicked from a toothbrush.

Using photographs on cold and rainy days

Used properly, photographs can be a useful adjunct to the painter. Personally I like to make my sketch from a photograph and then put the photograph away, otherwise I find myself tied to minute detail and untrue colours. It is better to be creative, in my opinion, and to decide for myself what colours I want to use. For example, a winter scene may be painted from a summer photograph and vice versa.

Painting from photographs is not as enjoyable as painting on the spot unless, of course, it is pouring with rain or freezing cold with a gale blowing. At these times, if you have the urge to paint a landscape, it is less hazardous to do so in a warm and comfortable studio.

I try always to carry a small camera with me. One never knows when a paintable subject may appear, but so often it occurs when time is too limited to paint or even sketch. It is also handy to have a camera to record different angles and aspects of a subject to keep on file for future reference.

When working from photographs you can develop just a small detail into a complete picture. Here I have outlined part of a photograph which I hope to develop, which is actually the focal point of the whole picture. First I work out the composition in a rough sketch, then I make the painting.

Bridge over the Grand Union

Size: 26cm sq. (10½in. sq.)
Paper: Fine grained painting paper
Brushes: nos. 8, 4 hog-hair oil

This painting I developed in the studio from the rather poor photograph shown here. A poor photograph is often, I think, an advantage because one is less tempted to copy the colours of the photograph. Ideally black and white photographs are better, for they force one to be creative with colour.

To begin with, I make the sketch (below) from the photograph, and in the process somewhat change the format. I then put the photograph away.

This bridge was built over the Grand Union Canal between North Kilworth and Welford on the North-amptonshire/Leicestershire border. The sole purpose was to connect fields on opposite sides of the canal for the passing of animals and farm traffic.

Before I put the drawing on to the canvas I prime it with yellow ochre and white to give the whole painting a glow, and to help convey the feeling of a sunny November afternoon.

After the wash is dry I apply the drawing and paint the sky with ultramarine blue, burnt sienna and white at the top, grading down to yellow ochre and white, while in places a little cadmium red is introduced, mixed with white to a pink colour. When I finish the sky I continue with the background, working from the furthest distance forward to the foreground.

When a painting contains water – a lake, river or canal – I always leave that element until last. I find that I then judge the values better and obtain the right contrast with the rest of the picture.

For the greens in the picture I use mixtures of sap green, ultramarine blue, burnt sienna and white. The trees are painted with burnt sienna, ultramarine blue, raw sienna, and white. The bridge and its reflection I paint with cadmium red, yellow ochre, and white. When the paint dries I add a tiny amount of sap green to give the impression of moss.

I find it very exciting to paint a landscape in the studio away from the actual scene. It gives me a freedom which I do not quite possess on the spot since I can see the detail so much more clearly when I am sitting only a few yards from my subject.

Photograph and sketch for the painting 'Bridge over the Grand Union' (opposite)

Over the hedge: demonstration (pages 25–6)

Acrylic painting used in traditional oil-painting technique

Size: 26¼cm sq. (10½in. sq.)
Paper: Fine grain oil-painting paper
Brushes: nos. 8, 4 oil brushes (hog-hair or nylon bristle); no. 1 rigger
Colours used: burnt sienna, ultramarine blue, sap green, yellow ochre, lemon yellow, and titanium white.

This painting (page 26) is composed in a style similar to the techniques used by oil painters, as is 'Surrey lane in winter'. It demonstrates flat, distant background in contrast with very detailed foreground.

Stage 1 (page 25)

I first give the canvas a wash of burnt sienna – this is using the colour mixed quite thinly with water. Painting your support with burnt sienna before you begin a landscape gives the picture a warm earthy glow. It also provides a warm contrasting red on which to place your green colours.

After the wash is dry I place my horizon line and paint the sky, for which I use ultramarine blue, burnt sienna, and white. When the white clouds are dry I mix a little yellow ochre with white and apply it to one side of the clouds – the sunny side. Even clouds have a light and dark side.

Stage 2

The distant church and trees I paint with a mixture of sap green and ultramarine blue, with white. The whole of the distant background is painted in a deliberately flat style. Distance, as I pointed out under 'Perspective', cuts down on brilliance of colour and detail. The fields and hedges are painted with the same three colours, although I add slightly more sap green.

Stage 3

I now paint in the middle ground hedge and cornfields; first the hedge, dark, with a mixture of sap green, ultramarine blue and burnt sienna. I then add a little white to this mixture to add a second, light value (two values for the middle ground, a little more detail than in the distance).

The cornfield is painted with a mixture of yellow ochre and white. A few detail strokes are added in the front with the no. 1 rigger, using ultramarine blue and burnt sienna.

Stage 4

Here I add very vigorous brush strokes to the foreground with mixtures of sap green, burnt sienna, ultramarine blue and yellow ochre.

Stage 5 – the finished painting (page 26)

To complete the painting I add finer detail to the foreground, introducing white mixed with the colours from the previous stage. I also add more detail to the cornfield, but make sure not to put in too much light detail along the bottom edge of the painting or in the corners because this could drag the viewer's eye away from the real focus of the painting.

Stage 1

Stage 2

Stage 3

Stage 4

25

Stage 5 – the finished painting
26

The gardener: demonstration (pages 28–9)

The individual characteristics of acrylics

Size: 26¼cm sq. (10½in. sq.)
Paper: Fine grain oil-painting paper
Brushes: nos. 8 and 4 hog-hair oil (or nylon acrylic); no. 1 rigger
Colours used: ultramarine blue, burnt sienna, cadmium red, sap green, raw sienna, lemon yellow and titanium white.

This painting demonstrates the individual characteristics and advantages of acrylic in building up a painting, in the use of glazes, and also in the addition of a figure to a landscape.

Stage 1 (page 28)

This sketch was made from two different sources. The gateway, roads and surroundings were drawn when I was on holiday in Devon in a little place at the mouth of the Dart river. The figure of the gardener was taken from photographs that I had taken of a locally well-known character in my native village in Leicestershire. The two subjects thus brought together form an interesting study.

Stage 2

I first make a tracing of the whole sketch but transfer to the canvas only the main elements, the sky and the ground. I then fix a line with a thin mixture of burnt sienna and water. Next the sky colour is blocked in and completely painted.

Stage 3

I return the traced sketch to the canvas, transfer the background trees and houses, and paint them in.

Stage 4

Once again I overlay the tracing and add the gateway, the drive and the bushes to the painting. I make sure that the strongest colours and values (lights and darks) are kept for the foreground. Background colours and value will, of course, be softer with less contrast to create the illusion of distance.

Stage 5 – the finished painting (page 29)

I now trace the figure and add it to the painting, trying, as I do so, to keep the colours of the clothing in harmony with the rest of the painting. A figure or object painted in bright or totally different colours will appear to be floating in front of the rest of the painting instead of being part of the whole.

Because of the speed at which acrylic dries it is possible to build up a painting, as I have this one, in the space of a few hours. Another asset lies in the application of glazes, for these too can be added within a short period of time.

In this painting I have provided a glaze of ultramarine blue by washing over the whole background, sky, trees, and distant buildings to create a sense of greater distance. Blue, being a cool colour, causes the parts of the painting glazed with it to appear to recede. Orange, being the complementary colour to blue, is used as a glaze over the foreground to bring that forward.

Glazes can, of course, be used in any part of a painting to tone down, brighten or enrich, and they are very often applied over an opaque area.

Stage 1

Stage 2

Stage 3

28

Stage 4

Stage 5 – the finished painting

Finishing and presentation of acrylic paintings

It is not necessary to varnish an acrylic painting, but it does give the surface a more even look. Acrylic varnish, both matt and glossy, can be purchased. Acrylic painting medium can also be used as a varnish: when first applied it appears milky, but do not be alarmed for, as it dries, it will become completely clear.

Acrylic paintings which are painted in the watercolour technique look best framed – as does a watercolour – with a mount and framed under glass. When used as an oil medium acrylics look best with a heavier frame, and no mount or glass. The presentation of a painting is very important and framing should be thought about seriously, for there is nothing worse than a good painting in a bad frame (such as those, with odd exceptions, bought in a junk shop.)

The cost can be reduced by attending a class on framing at your local adult education centre and making your own: or by buying all the pieces (moulding – cut by framer) mount, glass, and backing etc., and assembling them yourself.

Conclusion

More so than any other medium, acrylic is very versatile. It is exciting to explore its possibilities, not only in the ways that I have suggested in this book, but even further.

Mix it with a gouache, for example; and use it for detail and highlights in a watercolour. Use it to make an underpainting for oils or pastels, as both adhere well to its surface. The great advantage of using it as an underpainting with oils is, of course, its drying time. Remember, however, that acrylic *cannot* be used *over* oil paint.

People still tend to think of acrylics as new and unknown and therefore they avoid them. They are also thought of as bright, giving a plastic, over-vivid look to a painting. As I have shown in this book they lend themselves particularly well to landscape painting, and it takes a very well trained eye to see that watercolour or oil has not been used .

ACKNOWLEDGEMENTS

First published in Great Britain in 1988
Search Press Limited,
Wellwood, North Farm Road,
Tunbridge Wells, Kent TN2 3DR

Reprinted 1993

Text drawings and paintings by Wendy Clouse

Text, illustrations, arrangement and typography
copyright©Search Press Limited 1988

Distributors to the art trade:

UK
Winsor & Newton,
Whitefriars Avenue, Wealdstone,
Harrow, Middlesex HA3 5RH

USA
ColArt Americas Inc.,
11 Constitution Avenue, P.O. Box 1396, Piscataway,
NJ 08855-1396

Arthur Schwartz & Co.,
234 Meads Mountain Road, Woodstock, NY 12498

Canada
Anthes Universal Limited,
341 Heart Lake Road South, Brampton, Ontario L6W 3K8

Australia
Max A. Harrel
P.O. Box 92, Burnley, Victoria 3121

Jasco Pty Limited
937-941 Victoria Road, West Ryde, N.S.W. 2114

New Zealand
Caldwell Wholesale Limited,
Wellington and Auckland

South Africa
Ashley & Radmore (Pty) Limited,
P.O. Box 2794, Johannesburg 2000

Trade Winds Press (Pty) Limited,
P.O. Box 20194, Durban North 4016

ISBN 0 85532 579 8

Typeset by Scribe Design, Gillingham, Kent, England
Printed in Spain by A.G.Elkar S.Coop, 48012 Bilbao

Time spent studying trees will always be of great advantage to the landscape painter. It is important, however, to see the tree as a round mass, and not flat. Branches extend not only to the sides as many a student or amateur will accurately paint; they extend 'back-away' and also protrude towards the viewer. This requires some thought as the fore-shortened branches are not easy to draw.